C000089486

Venite Adoremus!

Venite Adoremus!

a series of daily reflections for Advent

FRAN GODFREY

McCrimmons
Great Wakering, Essex, England

My gratitude goes once again to Mgr Frederick Miles
for his homilies and debates
which have contributed to providing the seeds
for many of the ideas expressed in these Reflections.

First published in 2003 in the United Kingdom by
McCrimmon Publishing Co. Ltd.
10-12 High Street, Great Wakering, Essex SS3 0EQ
mccrimmons@dial.pipex.com
www.mccrimmons.com

Text © 2003 Fran Godfrey

ISBN 0 85597 651 9

Scripture quotations are taken from:
The Jerusalem Bible, published and copyright 1966, 1967 & 1968 and
The New Jerusalem Bible published and copyright 1985 by
Darton, Longman & Todd Ltd and Doubleday & Co. Inc.,
a division of Random House, and used by permission;
New American Bible with Revised Psalms © 1991, 1986, 1970
Confraternity of Christian Doctrine, Washington, D.C.
and are used with permission of the copyright owner. All rights reserved.
No part of the *New American Bible* may be reproduced in any form
without permission in writing from the copyright holder.

Every effort has been made to trace the owners of copyright material,
and we hope that no copyright has been infringed. Pardon is sought and apologies made
if the contrary be the case, and a correction will be made in any reprint of this book.

Images © The Benedictine Sisters of Turvey Abbey
and Sr Mary Stephen
Cover design and layout by Nick Snode
Typeset in 11 & 12pt Palatino roman and 24pt Aesop
Text pages printed on 115gsm, cover printed on 280gsm one sided art
Printed and bound in England by Trafford Press, Doncaster

Contents

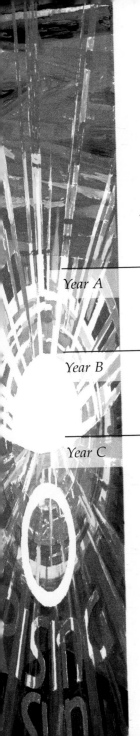

First Sunday of Advent

Year A

"The night is almost over, it will be daylight soon – let us give up all the things we prefer to do under cover of dark;"

Romans 13: 12

Year B

*"Be on your guard, stay awake, because you never know when the time will come.
… What I say to you I say to all: Stay awake!"*

Mark 13: 37

Year C

"Stay awake, praying at all times for the strength to survive all that is going to happen, and to stand with confidence before the Son of Man."

Luke 21: 36

TOMORROW, next week, next month won't do. The time to change, to amend our ways is now. Now. Take time; be honest; look deep inside yourself and know your shortcomings; identify your flaws. We all have faults. Maybe we have grown used to them; attached to them almost. We shrug them off – perhaps with a laugh: "I'm afraid I'm terribly impatient." "I've grown awfully selfish in my old age." "It was only a small white lie really." If we could cure ourselves of the vanity, selfishness, greed, jealousy and any number of other faults we may possess, then we would surely be cured of sin. Sinning is more a result of what we are, rather than the things we do. We do what we do because of the way we are. If we always, always acted with charity in our hearts and in our minds we would not sin.

Look for the good things in you and around you. How very much you have to be grateful for. Maybe life is not easy for you; you can be sure it is harder for someone else. There is always something to be thankful for. Most of all we can be thankful for our Faith. We know that – whatever happens to us – God is close at hand. If we submit to His will, He will carry us over the hurdles. Be certain of that.

The time to change is now. Tomorrow could be too late. If we try to change, try to follow Christ, our future in heaven is assured. Our future in this life is not. "Stay awake"; be ready. 'If only...' is one of the saddest phrases.

ॐ   My Lord and my God,
       make me ever wakeful to my need to change.
   Give me the vision to see your will for me
       and the strength to obey and serve you.
   Give me eyes to see the good around me;
       in your love, accept my gratitude for all that you
       have given me.
   Guard me and guide me and bring me ever closer to
       you; I am lost without you.

   Lord, fill me with your grace so that I may be ready to
       receive you with joy.
         Amen.

Monday

*"The centurion replied,
'Sir, I am not worthy to have
you under my roof; just give
the word and my servant will
be cured."*

Matthew 8: 8

WAS THERE EVER such an expression of faith? Even Our Lord – we are told by Saint Matthew – "was astonished" at the faith shown by the centurion. There are numerous examples throughout the gospels of Christ healing the sick and curing the diseased. The cures were all reliant on a degree of faith on the part of the afflicted, but in the majority of cases Our Lord was actually present with the person begging for cure. The faith of the centurion was so great that he believed Our Lord could heal his servant from a distance. What a remarkable man: a deeply kind person who cared for his servant to that extent; a humble person who felt, as a Roman, that his home was not a place for Christ to visit; and, above all a man who seemed not to question for an instant Christ's power and ability. How different from so many people from Our Lord's own background.

The centurion was, of course, rewarded, as we will be if we can display that level of faith and absolute trust in God's care for us.

ॐ My Lord and my God,
        I place all my trust in you.
      I believe that you will always care for me
        and never leave me to face life alone.
      I adore you my Lord, my Creator, my Redeemer,
        my life and my strength.

      Lord, fill me with your grace
        so that I may be ready to receive you with joy.
        Amen.

Tuesday

"Filled with joy by the Holy Spirit, Jesus said, 'I bless you Father, Lord of heaven and earth ...'"

Luke 10: 21

PEOPLE aren't always very sure about the Holy Spirit. We can be good at praying to God the Father because we can recognise and accept Him as our Creator and the Creator of the Universe. We know more about God the Son than about any member of the Blessed Trinity because He was the one who became one of us, who taught us as God-made-Man. He is God's Word made human; Christ is the instrument God used to put His message across to a sinful world and the means of our salvation through obedience to the point of death. But when it comes to the Holy Spirit we tend not to be quite so sure. We are told He appeared as tongues of fire and a strong wind, but that doesn't really make it easy for us to worship Him as part of the Trinity.

And yet the Holy Spirit is vital for our salvation. It is the Holy Spirit who comes to us at Baptism and Confirmation; the Holy Spirit who dwells in our souls and gives us our conscience, our strength, our inspiration, our ability to believe and understand the sacred. If we achieve any level of holiness, that is the indwelling of the Holy Spirit. Think of how we sometimes describe people as 'kind-spirited' or 'mean-spirited' and how we indicate in those ways the very fundamental characteristics of a fellow human being. Someone's spirit is the essence of their being. If we manage to be filled with the Holy Spirit we will indeed be filled with joy.

℘ O Blessed Spirit
       come to me and live deep within me.
     Fill me with your grace, your goodness,
       your strength and your truth.
     Take root within my being
       and guide and protect me always.

     Lord, fill me with your grace
       so that I may be ready to receive you with joy.
         Amen.

Wednesday

*"The Lord is my Shepherd;
there is nothing I shall want."*
Psalm 23 (22)

HERE ARE NUMEROUS references in the gospels to Our Lord being a shepherd and we His sheep. The analogy was not wasted on the people of Christ's time as so many of the community were shepherds or fishermen. They knew about sheep and about caring for them. Most of us probably know very little about sheep apart from the fact that they appear to be quite silly animals and, of course, that they follow each other aimlessly. That could sum us up, too. Man today is so obsessed with possessions, with owning what his neighbour has – only perhaps a better one. We strive to earn more to possess more. And those who have little or nothing can sometimes turn to crime to possess what they think they have a right to. There is always something new, something better, something more expensive and exclusive to aim at. If only we could really absorb the truth of how transitory it all is. How there is nothing in this world that counts for anything if we ignore God. We have been given a beautiful world and man has invented and built many things from God-given resources to make us all more comfortable. And there is nothing wrong with living comfortably. It is when the pursuit of riches and possessions takes over our lives to the exclusion of what is really important – love of God and love and care for our neighbour – that we are in grave danger. If we sheep listen to the words of our Shepherd, and follow where He leads, there is nothing we shall want.

ॐ My Lord and my God,
    without you I am foolish and lost.
Shine a light for me in the darkness,
    draw me ever closer to you
    and keep me safely by your side.
May I never forget that all things come from you
    and are gifts to be used wisely and charitably.

Lord, fill me with your grace
    so that I may be ready to receive you with joy.
        Amen.

Thursday

"It is not those who say to me, 'Lord, Lord', who will enter the kingdom of heaven, but the person who does the will of my Father in heaven."
Matthew 7: 21

THE ACCUSATION levelled frequently at church-goers (and perhaps Catholics more than any other) is that of 'Hypocrites!' We are accused of attending Mass and going to church regularly, and yet behaving in a way which gives the lie to what we are supposed to believe. And, to be fair, there *are* cases of church-goers who go to Holy Mass as a matter of habit, and then step outside the church and behave spitefully, jealously, impatiently, unkindly or selfishly – without ever seeing the incongruity of their behaviour.

On the other hand there are those of us who are sinners. Who go to church and attend Mass regularly – and are very fully aware of our faults and flaws. Christ, the Divine Physician, came to heal the sick, to call sinners to Him – and, let's be honest, that means us. And that is the precise reason we go into a church. We know that alone we cannot conquer our sinfulness, and we throw ourselves on the mercy of our loving Father. We accept that the only goodness inside us is the presence of God's Spirit, God's grace, and we plead for the strength to do the will of our Almighty Father.

ॐ My Lord and my God,
        help me to see how and where I go wrong
        and offend you.
    Grant me the strength to do your will
        so that I may be with you one day
        in your eternal kingdom of peace and joy.
    May I never fail to cry out to you
        in humility and adoration.

    Lord, fill me with your grace
        so that I may be ready to receive you with joy.
            Amen.

Friday

*"The Lord is my light and my help; whom shall I fear?
The Lord is the stronghold of my life; before whom shall I shrink?"*

Psalm 27 (26)

AS LONG AS OUR LIVES are grounded in ourselves and our own abilities, we are sure to be disappointed. We make wrong decisions, we act uncharitably, we hurt others and get hurt ourselves. If we place our trust in human beings, there is a good chance we will be let down at some point. Very few people are completely selfless and act altruistically all of the time. Many people have some sort of 'agenda' or axe to grind. It's the way we are. To meet a truly selfless person is to meet a saint in the making. If our lives are grounded – truly centred – on God, we have nothing to fear. His love for us is complete and absolute. Which doesn't mean that we are safeguarded from all unpleasantness or pain, it means that whatever comes our way, we will get through it if our gaze remains steadily fixed on God. Consider that it is generally accepted that the worst that can happen to us in this life, is death. And yet if our lives are centred on God, on following His commands and obeying His will – death holds no fear for us. We have only a wonderful, everlasting life to look forward to. At home for ever.

ᘚ☞ My Lord and my God,
>   keep me from fear and pointless worry.
>   May I treat every hardship that comes my way
>   >   as a lesson to be learned in following you
>   >   more nearly.
>   Grant me the strength to manage and
>   >   the vision to see that you are always nearby
>   >   watching over me and loving me.
>
>   Lord, fill me with your grace
>   >   so that I may be ready to receive you with joy.
>   >   Amen.

Saturday

"The harvest is rich but the labourers are few, so ask the Lord of the harvest to send labourers to his harvest."
Matthew 9: 37

'MONEY CAN'T BUY HAPPINESS' is a cliché – but like most clichés it has truth at its centre. So often we hear of people who want for nothing material, but who still feel that something is missing from their lives. We read daily in our newspapers of millionaire 'celebrities' who have deeply unhappy lives and turn to drink and drugs as a means of escape, and we may feel that if we had what they had, we would be happy. But it is unlikely in the long term. We have been made in the image and likeness of our Creator. We have a part of Him deep within us, in our souls, and this part cries out to be heard and united with our God. We are loved deeply and we need to love in return. So many people try hard to ignore that call, that tiny seed within each of us, and that is what leads to unhappiness. The world is crying out for it knows not what. So indeed the harvest is rich. The prayer we need to make is that the Lord will send His Spirit to inspire more labourers to work for Him. And that we will

have the wisdom, courage and understanding to admit the Spirit
when He comes to us.

୧ⅽ My Lord and my God,
        open the hearts and minds of your people
        to receive your Holy Spirit
        so that your world may be converted and saved.
    It is your divine will that those you have created
        out of love may one day be reunited with you
        in heaven.
    Open our ears to hear your word,
        and our minds to receive it with gratitude.
    Guide and inspire your labourers
        to work lovingly and honestly for you.

    Lord, fill me with your grace
        so that I may be ready to receive you with joy.
        Amen.

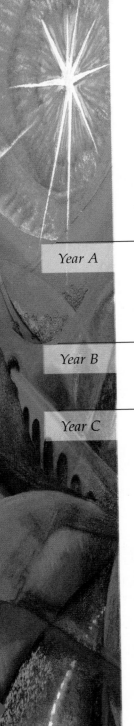

Second Sunday of Advent

Year A

"May he who helps us when we refuse to give up, help you all to be tolerant with each other, following the example of Christ Jesus, so that united in mind and voice you may give glory to God the Father."

Romans 15: 5

Year B

"Prepare in the wilderness a way for the Lord. Make a straight highway for our God across the desert."

Isaiah 40: 3

Year C

"My prayer is that your love for each other may increase more and more and never stop improving your knowledge and deepening your perception so that you can always recognise what is best. This will help you to become pure and blameless ..."

Philippians 1: 9

N O ONE – believer or non-believer – could deny that the world around us is quite simply beautiful. Sometimes we can fail to see the wood for the trees. We focus on the problems around us and fail to see the wider splendour of the world. We complain about litter on the streets, and ignore the perfection of the rose in the garden. We bemoan the congestion on our motorways, and ignore the soaring mountains, the rolling hills, the breathtaking trees. The things we complain about are man-made. God created perfection for us. Does He now look in despair at the wilderness we have made of His creation, I wonder? Man has done much that is good and that has often been when he has been trying to help his fellow man. Things that have been done out of selfishness and greed have corroded the beauty of the world of which we have been given stewardship. Created in the image of God, man has such potential for good and yet our inability to look further than this life leads us to seek wealth and position, which will count for nothing in so very short a time.

Love and consideration for everyone else, treating every person with respect, helping one another and putting God first, our neighbour second and ourselves last will give us the courage to face God as pure and blameless beings; as creatures who have tried to repent and straighten a path through the tangled wilderness we have made of His world.

ℬ☞ My Lord and my God, may I never forget to thank you
    for the beauty of the world around me.
When trivial problems press in on my small world,
    help me to see past them and remember always that
    everything in this life passes.
Let me build a straight path to you, and never stray
    from it, but always fix my sights on the glory of
    eternal life with you. I truly repent of all the pain
    I have caused you and beseech you to break down
    the barrier of sin which I erect between myself and
    your grace so lovingly offered to me.

    Lord, fill me with your grace
        so that I may be ready to receive you with joy.
        Amen.

Monday

"Which of these is easier to say, 'Your sins are forgiven you', or to say, 'Get up and walk'?"

Luke 5: 23

I HAVE A NON-BELIEVER FRIEND who said to me once: "Show me the proof and then I'll believe." That would not be faith; that would be knowledge. Again and again we read in the gospels of the importance of faith, and the great store Our Lord sets by faith. How often did He reward faith; how often did He tell his disciples and followers that anyone who believed in Him would be saved. And yet still He was asked for proof of who He said He was.

In this instance, Our Lord gives the people proof. But not just proof that He could heal and cure, but proof that He had the power of forgiveness, by first forgiving the paralytic his sins, and THEN curing his paralysis – as an outwardly visible sign of His power.

We don't have the advantage of walking with God-made-Man and witnessing His power in such a physical way. But we do have the advantage of hindsight. We know how He died and how He rose again as He said He would; that is the only proof we need. The evidence is there before us; the power to believe is a gift and is in our hands.

☞ My Lord and my God,
    I believe and I thank you for the gift
      of my belief.
  Strengthen me in my faith and
    banish any doubts I may have about your Truth.
  May I live my life in such a way as to please you
    and merit the reward you have promised
    to those who believe.

  Lord, fill me with your grace
    so that I may be ready to receive you with joy.
    Amen.

Tuesday

"Suppose a man has a hundred sheep, and one of them strays; will he not leave the ninety-nine on the hillside and go in search of the stray?"

Matthew 18: 12

HOW COMFORTING a thought that is. We are all weak. We all stray so very often. In this life if we offend our fellow-man, he is unlikely to come looking for us to draw us into friendship with him. He is far more likely to abandon us completely with the comment 'Good riddance'. How hard it is to imagine someone loving us as much as the Lord does. We sin against Him; we offend or disappoint Him and instead of abandoning us to our fate, He comes after us. He will never force us back into His fold, because we have the great gift of free will. But He will come looking for us; He will reach out and offer us forgiveness – again and again. He will look for the smallest sign of repentance on our part, and then He will rejoice because we are no longer lost. So much love when we are so undeserving. It's one of the hardest things for us to understand, believe and accept.

꒰☜ My Lord and my God,
     I know that I stray often from you.
    Please never stop looking for me.
  Grant me the humility to repent and
      accept your grace,
       your love and your forgiveness.
  Strengthen my will to follow you and
      keep me from straying from the safety
        of your protection.

Lord, fill me with your grace
    so that I may be ready to receive you with joy.
     Amen.

Wednesday

"My soul, give thanks to the
Lord, all my being bless his
holy name. My soul give
thanks to the Lord and never
forget all his blessings."

Psalm 103 (102)

A S A RACE, we human beings are better at finding fault
than feeling gratitude. Our problems and ills loom large
in our minds, and we take for granted all the good and
wonderful things in our lives. I suppose it's under-
standable. Pain, for instance, tends to overwhelm most other
feelings. 'Buck-you-up' friends tell us to remember that "there is
always someone worse off than you". Which is almost certainly
true, but not necessarily that helpful in assuaging pain and illness.
And yet it is another way of saying – count your blessings;
remember the good things. Look around you at the world, and
marvel at its splendour and beauty. Consider the great and good
things man has achieved (by the grace of God) in his quest to make
life more comfortable. Think of the people who care about you and
for whom you care.

Remember the great gift that is the ability to love and feel
compassion. Stand in awe and wonder at the order of nature – the

workings of the human body and brain – and although man does involve himself, it would all happen without his interference.

However hard it may sometimes be to feel cheerful, day always, always, follows night. Remember to feel gratitude and to give thanks to God that He has seen you through the darkness, as He certainly will if you place yourself in His hands. Never forget all His blessings.

ॐ My Lord and my God,
>   I give you thanks for all the wonderful things
>   in my life.
>   May I never take for granted the beauty around me
>   and the gifts you have given me,
>   and may I always use these to your greater
>   glory.

>   Lord, fill me with your grace
>   so that I may be ready to receive you with joy.
>   Amen.

Thursday

> *"Of all the children born of women, a greater than John the Baptist has never been seen; yet the least in the kingdom of heaven is greater than he is."*
>
> Matthew 11: 11

*O*UR LORD loved his cousin John greatly. They had 'bonded' before either was born. When Our Lady, carrying in her womb the Son of God, went to visit her cousin, Elizabeth had declared that her baby had leapt with joy. The adult John then gave up all prospects of an easy, comfortable life and went to live a life of hardship and deprivation in the wilderness. A wild and passionate man, feeding on what was available in the desert and proclaiming tirelessly his message of repentance in preparation for the coming of the Redeemer. From what we read in the gospels, we can infer that he was a man of great humility. He resisted all attempts to be lionised and hailed as a great prophet, declaring always that he was only there to prepare the way for the One who was to follow – who would baptise, not with water, but with the Holy Spirit and whose sandal-strap he was not worthy to undo. He was a man with a message and a great determination to proclaim that message – and he clearly made much impact as even Herod's conscience was goaded by his preaching, to the point of reluctance to have him beheaded. It was Herod's pride and John's denunciation of the King's evil lifestyle which resulted in the Baptist's martyrdom.

'And yet the least in the kingdom of heaven is greater than he is'. However much we achieve on earth, it is not until we reach our heavenly destination – our proper home with our Creator – that we will gain our full potential; be made perfect and with that perfection will come the supreme happiness for which we long.

✎   My Lord and my God,
            grant me the humility and dedication of
               St John the Baptist.
       May I never fear to speak out in your defence
            nor fail to spread your Truth by word and deed.
       In your mercy, guide me in this life
            so that I may attain a place in your kingdom
               when you call me.

       Lord, fill me with your grace
            so that I may be ready to receive you with joy.
               Amen.

Friday

> *"We played the pipes for you,*
> *and you would not dance; we*
> *sang dirges, and you*
> *wouldn't be mourners."*
>
> Matthew 11: 17

W E HAVE PROBABLY all met the type of person who is determined to be difficult. No matter what we do, it is wrong. That sort of contrary person can be very tiring to be with. It can sometimes be associated with increasing age. We can get grumpy and refuse to be cheered up. We focus on our problems and turn our back on the good parts of our life, preferring to wallow in self-pity – that can be such a comfortable and self-indulgent pool and one it is easy to sink into.

We see here Our Lord showing slight exasperation with the people around Him. They complained because the Baptist acted unusually in not indulging in food and drink; and when Our Lord acted normally in eating and drinking with, not only his friends, but also with sinners, they accused Him of being a glutton. There is always a cloud within the silver lining, and some people are adept at finding the cloud and ignoring the lining. They bend all the facts to fit the interpretation they wish to place on any action or word. It isn't difficult to do. The hard thing is to see beyond the trivial to the Truth. Christ and John the Baptist had a message to convey; their listeners were determined not to hear, but to dwell only on the inconsequential. We never would, would we?

⁖ My Lord and my God,

> grant me the vision to discern your truth
> and to set aside that which is of no
> importance.

May I always be able to see past the unimportant
> and see clearly what you desire of me,
> then grant me the strength to follow your will.

Lord, fill me with your grace
> so that I may be ready to receive you with joy.
> Amen.

Saturday

"God of hosts, bring us back;
let your face shine on us and
we shall be saved."

Psalm 80 (79)

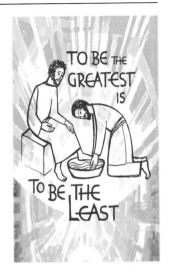

MAN TODAY LIKES TO THINK he is completely self-sufficient. People pride themselves on being able to manage. And 'pride' is the operative word there. We sometimes hear it: "He has too much pride to ask for help." "I won't take handouts." "I don't need charity." It requires a great deal of humility to accept our weakness and our dependence on others. There is a great deal of difference between scrounging or laziness, and admitting we just can't manage without some help. And this sort of fierce independence seems to be something we are born with. Most mothers can tell stories of how their toddlers refuse to be helped when it comes – for example – to putting their shoes on the right feet, or doing up the buttons on a shirt!

And it requires great humility to turn to God and say "I have got it wrong; I have made a serious mistake; I have sinned." And then even more humility to acknowledge that we simply cannot put it right, or be forgiven without His help. We need to learn to show true penitence, accept full blame for our sinfulness, and to admit that we have sinned because we have turned away from God into darkness, away from His face which shines on us giving us light and strength. God will never refuse to forgive the honest and genuine penitent. And, knowing our weakness, He will continue to do so every time we turn to Him in remorse and humility. God will always reach out to save those who genuinely want to be saved.

೭☚ My Lord and my God,
> without you I am lost.
> I am weak and sinful and I know that
>> I often fall away from your grace in my pride
>>> by turning from your will.
> I beseech you, do not despair of me,
>> how ever often I despair of myself.
> I know that I need your help to be stronger;
> I can do nothing good or be no one good without
>> you.

> Lord, fill me with your grace
>> so that I may be ready to receive you with joy.
>>> Amen.

Third Sunday of Advent (Gaudete)

Year A

"Strengthen all weary hands, steady all trembling knees and say to all faint hearts, "Courage! Do not be afraid. Look, your God is coming ... he is coming to save you."

Isaiah 35: 3

Year B

"Be happy at all times; pray constantly; and for all things give thanks to God. ... God has called you and he will not fail you."

Thessalonians 5: 16; 24

Year C

"If anyone has two tunics he must share with the man who has none, and the one with something to eat must do the same."

Luke 3: 11

TODAY is known as Gaudete Sunday – the Sunday in Advent for special rejoicing. I don't think we do rejoice much these days. The pleasures we seek are so very short-lived that we barely have time to rejoice before they are spent. Maybe we feel that there is nothing much to rejoice about. The longer man inhabits this world, the more problems he seems to create for himself and others. We approach life from the wrong perspective.

We tend to look for what life can give to us, rather than what we can contribute. We would prefer to hang on to both our tunics, just in case – rather than share what we have. Real happiness comes from deep goodness. So many of the saints had lives filled with hardship, and yet you never hear of a miserable saint. To do God's will is to find true happiness. Fighting against it is to find struggle and misery. We must accept our condition and our situation. And never forget to pray. We must keep in constant contact with our Father, trusting that He will always hear our prayers and answer them in the light of His complete knowledge of us. We are urged to trust Our Lord – and trust can be so hard because we only have experience of trusting human beings and that can so often lead to hurt and disappointment. Be patient. Remember always that God can never let us down. Never.

☙ My Lord and my God,
> I rejoice that you created me
>> and that you continue to hold me in existence.
> I rejoice in the knowledge that, though I am a
>> sinner, you are the means of my salvation.
> I give thanks for those who love me, care for me,
>> care about me.
> Teach me patience and generosity.
> Help me to understand that everything I have
>> comes from you and that if I succeed in being
>> generous, it is you who is working through me.
> I trust that through your love and your mercy,
>> my God, I may be with you one day.
>
> Lord, fill me with your grace
>> so that I may be ready to receive you with joy.
>> Amen.

Monday

'Jesus said, "I will ask you a question: John's baptism: what was its origin, heavenly or human? ... Their reply to Jesus was, "We do not know." Jesus retorted, "Nor will I tell you my authority for acting like this." '

Matthew 21: 24,27

MONG ALL OF GOD'S CREATION, Man alone was created a rational being. We were given a brain with the ability to think deeply, consider, make reasoned decisions. We have a soul which provides us with the ability to feel emotion – love, hate, anger, jealousy, pride. And we were given, above all, free will – the ability to choose what we think, what we do. And what we believe. Jesus was often asked for proof of who He was and of what right He had to teach what He did. Even one of His own followers, Philip – a believer – asked Him to "Show us the Father." (Jonn 14: 8). Once again Our Lord emphasised the importance of absolute faith. He could have provided any amount of proof of who He was; but that would make the gifts of faith and free will meaningless. In the same way, Almighty God could intervene to prevent all disasters, accidents, catastrophes, but then Man would never take responsibility for himself and his actions if he knew that God would always 'bale him out'. Just about everything we do has some effect on someone and we have to learn to be accountable and responsible – not just for ourselves, but for the consequences of our actions and their effect on others.

In this extract from St Matthew's gospel Our Lord is challenging the elders in the Temple to think for themselves. To listen to His teaching, to consider its truth and to make their own decisions about His authority. Just as in a good 'whodunnit' – all the clues are there to enable everyone to come to the right conclusion.

• My Lord and my God,
>   I offer you my thanks for all the gifts you have
>   given me:
>   my ability to reason, to believe and to love.
>   Send the Holy Spirit to me
>   to inspire and guide me to your truth.
>   Grant that I may please you in my every thought,
>   word and deed.
>
>   Fill me with your grace so
>   that I may be ready to receive you with joy.
>   Amen.

Tuesday

"Jesus said, 'I tell you solemnly, tax collectors and prostitutes are making their way into the kingdom of God before you."

Matthew 21: 31

A S CHRISTIANS we might sometimes be tempted to think we have got the right answer, and rest on our laurels. And we know from reading our daily newspapers that all sorts of so-called religious people make mistakes – sometimes horrifically sinful mistakes. And we wonder how on earth anybody – let alone clergy and religious – can go so terribly wrong. Of course, it is because they are tempted as we all are; they are weak and sinful as we all are. And sometimes it is easy to hide behind a bright veneer of righteousness and holiness. It has always been so – in Our Lord's time on earth He frequently accused the supposedly good and holy members of the Jewish faith – the scribes, the elders – of hypocrisy. They were so busy observing the letter of the law and trying to protect their own positions in society, that they failed to obey the spirit of the law, to respond to and obey God's absolute law of charity. They could not see that they were sinners and needed forgiveness and help. Whereas the simpler people listened with eagerness – they heard Our Lord describe what was right and good and they recognised themselves as sinners and wrong-doers. Once they had arrived at that realisation it was a short step to penitence and amendment. We need to think carefully about which camp we are in.

☙ My Lord and my God,
　　　　help me to recognise my sinfulness
　　　　　　and identify my weaknesses.
　　　Let me see myself in an honest light and,
　　　　with your help,
　　　　　　work towards removing my faults.
　　　Open my ears to hear your word
　　　　　and strengthen my ability to act on it.

　　　Fill me with your grace
　　　　　so that I may be ready to receive you with joy.
　　　　　　Amen.

Wednesday

"Happy is the man who does not lose faith in me."

Luke 19: 23

GAIN AND AGAIN we come back to the same theme – that of the importance of faith in the Lord God. It would be helpful if, once we had studied 'the evidence' and decided to believe what was written in the Gospels, we were forever after assured of having a strong faith. But of course that doesn't always happen. Our faith can be tried often – and sometimes sorely. We can be assailed by all sorts of doubts, not least because the society in which we live is such a very secular one. It is much easier to believe in nothing but yourself and your right to happiness, at all costs. Sometimes our non-believer friends seem to be having a much more comfortable life, with their undisturbed consciences and their Sunday mornings in bed; are we sure that, as we struggle with our attempts at self-denial and rejection of what we are taught is sinful – that we haven't got it all wrong? Satan is skilled at disguise and is well able to hide his blackened interior under a glossy coat of attractiveness.

It is much easier to maintain our faith while all is going well. It is when tragedy or hardship strike us or those we love that it can be easy to be hurt and angry with God for 'allowing this to happen'. That is when we are most tested. Again, it is a case of turning to God, accepting what has happened and that we may not understand the whys and wherefores, and asking for God's help in carrying on. It is not the time to lose our trust in God. Without our faith we will indeed be desolate. Only God has the power to comfort and, ultimately, to wipe away every tear.

༂☞ My Lord and my God,
> I believe; keep strong my belief.
> When sufferings come to me, be especially near
> and save me from doubts and misgivings.
> I trust in your bountiful love and mercy
> and know that one day I shall understand,
> if it is your will.

> Fill me with your grace
> so that I may be ready to receive you with joy.
> Amen.

Thursday

*"I will praise you, Lord,
you have rescued me."*

Psalm 29

OW GOOD are we at thanking God? Our prayers probably consist of a fairly long list of requests – not just for ourselves, of course; but also for those we love and care for, and – when we remember – for things like peace in the world, an end to starvation, drought and disease in the Third World. Sometimes, when things don't seem to improve and our own personal world remains full of troubles, we may wonder if it is worth our while continuing to pray. And yet, most of us do continue. We have read and believe that we have to persevere with our prayers. Consider the great perseverance of Saint Monica who prayed ceaselessly for the conversion of her son, Saint Augustine. It took 30 years for her prayers to be answered. God does hear us, but He clearly has His reasons for delaying His response, or apparently denying some of our requests. At times like those, we need to try and consider what lesson we are being asked to learn.

On many occasions our prayers are answered in the way we would like them to be. People recover from illness; our children pass exams; we secure that new job; certain worries prove groundless. On all such occasions are we quite sure that – in among all our rejoicing and celebration – we remember to offer grateful thanks to God, who has heard our prayers? Do we remember to thank God regularly for the gift of our faith, and, thereby, our means of salvation? As we meditate on the Crucifix, do we remember not only to hang our heads in shame that we caused such an atrocity, but also to thank Our Lord for what He went through to rescue us?

℞   My Lord and my God,
>   may I never forget to thank you
>>   for all the many gifts you have given me,
>>   for the beauty of your creation around me and,
>>   above all, for the sacrifice of your life to save
>>   mine.
>   I offer you here and now my gratitude and love,
>>   and pray that you will accept these
>>>   and forgive me for all the times I forget.

>   Fill me with your grace
>>   so that I may be ready to receive you with joy.
>>   Amen.

Friday

*"The works my Father has
given me to carry out, these
same works of mine testify
that the Father has sent me."*
John 5: 36

I DO WONDER SOMETIMES how the people in the time that Christ was on earth, could have failed to believe who He was. Surely no normal human being could effect the cures He effected. Over and again we read in the gospels of how Our Lord was able, with a word, to cure long-standing diseases, deformity, blindness and lameness. He even allowed His great friend Lazarus to remain buried for three days after his death, before going to him and bringing him back to life. How could the onlookers doubt that this man was who He said He was – the Son of God? I suppose it shows that if you are determined not to believe, if what you are being asked to believe rocks your own little world, makes you look at how you are living and forces you to admit that you must change to be saved – if you are that determined to protect yourself from all that – then you will refuse to believe. Certainly today it is much easier to ignore the writings of those who lived alongside Our Lord during His life on earth.

It is easy to find any number of excuses to doubt. We live in a world where science can prove so much; we are used to being provided with evidence as to why certain things happen; scientists can satisfactorily explain so many phenomena. So if rock-solid proof cannot be provided as to, for example, the Resurrection of Our Lord – then it can't possibly have happened, say those who will only reason so far and refuse to have their comfortable notions disturbed.

Thanks be to God for our faith.

ॐ My Lord and my God,
> I pray that you may send the Holy Spirit
>> to enlighten the eyes and minds of those who
>>> will not believe.
> May I bear witness to you in everything that I say
>> and do and thereby offer some small sign of
>>> proof of your existence in me.

> Lord, fill me with your grace
>> so that I may be ready to receive you with joy.
>>> Amen.

Fourth Sunday of
Advent

Year A

"Take Mary home as your wife, because she has conceived what is in her by the Holy Spirit. She will give birth to a son and you must name him Jesus, because he is the one who is to save his people from their sins."

Matthew 1: 21

Year B

"The Holy Spirit will come upon you ... and the power of the Most High will cover you with its shadow. And so the child will be holy and will be called the Son of God."

Luke 1: 35

Year C

"Blessed is she who believed that the promise made her by the Lord would be fulfilled."

Luke 1: 44

I DON'T THINK anyone disputes that a man called Jesus was born and lived about 2000 years ago. Many people accept that he was 'a great prophet' and a good man who lived by and taught a sublime moral code. But people do have a problem with Jesus being the Son of God. And also with the Virgin Birth. If you have ever seen pictures of a tiny baby, newly conceived, in the womb surely you cannot doubt the ability of God to perform miracles. When the baby is the size of a walnut it is already starting to grow limbs and beginning to take on the shape of a human being. This tiny creature comes from a fertilised egg, gradually grows into the most complex of entities – far above and beyond anything man can invent – and God performs this miracle for man and woman millions and millions of times over. Would it really be such a problem for the Almighty Creator to will the planting of a seed of a baby in the womb of a woman? As to whether or not this man was the Son of God, that is a matter of pure faith, based on what we read in the Gospels and whether or not we accept the truth of what was written by a group of men who moved and lived with Christ. Remember how they believed He was their King and their Saviour? Remember how afraid and disillusioned they were when He was taken from them and crucified in the manner reserved for the lowest of society? Remember how they themselves were re-born into new and powerful preachers after the Resurrection? Remember how they went to their martyrs' death rather than deny the Truth. A man will not die for a whim or something which might be possible. Truly this was the Son of God. Mary knew it; the disciples knew it. And you and I know it.

ℰ❧ My Lord and my God,
      may I learn the absolute obedience of Mary
         as she accepted without question your will for her.
Jesus, my Lord,
      teach me to follow God's will as you did,
         out of perfect love.
O, Holy Spirit,
      make your home in me: inspire me, direct me,
         sustain me and fill me with grace,
            love and fortitude.

Lord, fill me with your grace
      so that I may be ready to receive you with joy.
        Amen.

17 December

"Abraham was the father of Isaac, Isaac the father of Jacob ..."

Matthew 1: 1

T HIS PART of Saint Matthew's gospel lists the names of the forty-two generations leading up to the birth of Jesus Christ, born of Mary who was the wife of Joseph of the House of David.

Names and heredity were very important in the Jewish culture. In a number of instances God changed the names of the forefathers: Abram became Abraham, Jacob became Israel, for example. Family was, and still is, central to the Jewish people. To give birth to a baby was a great blessing, and women who were unable to conceive were regarded in some way as having been displeasing to God, of being punished. Remember how Elizabeth rejoiced and thanked God when, even at an advanced age, she conceived and gave birth to John the Baptist ("The Lord has done this for me ... it has pleased him to take away the humiliation I suffered among men." Luke 1: 25)

Would that our society today always treated pregnancy and babies with such joy, gratitude and love. Sex is now largely seen as a recreation – like going to the theatre, or eating out at a restaurant. It is regarded as a means for man and woman to satisfy their lust and their desire for pleasure, without any thought for the prime purpose or wishing to take responsibility for the possible consequences. Whether or not a person believes in God, surely the most wonderful thing that can happen in this world is for two people to fall deeply in love and to want to join together in such a way that they become as one, and then to crown that love by being able to give birth to a baby – a fusion of both parents, being part of both parents and a celebration of their love for one another. Of course there are millions of loving couples who do have this attitude. But there are also millions of people (and young children even) who are interested in nothing more than self-gratification; they want pleasure only – whether it comes from a pint of lager, a fillet steak or sex. The result is a complete degradation of sex and cavalier disregard for life. On the one hand there are thousands of abortions performed every week; on the other hand, women of all ages are desperate to have children – leading to babies being created in test-tubes, and – if some scientists have their way – from the cells of dead foetuses. Can this really be what God had in mind when He created us and gave us the gift to continue in a special way His work of creation?

℘ My Lord and my God,
forgive us for our selfish and greedy attitude to the
great gifts you have given us.
May mankind learn again the meaning of true selfless love
and come to respect once more the blessed gift of life
from its earliest beginnings to its last breath.

Lord, fill me with your grace
so that I may be ready to receive you with joy.
Amen.

18 December

"Joseph, son of David, do not be afraid to take Mary home as your wife, because she has conceived what is in her by the Holy Spirit."

Matthew 1: 20

WE KNOW SO VERY LITTLE about Saint Joseph. We know he was a carpenter, because Jesus is referred to by his own people as "the carpenter's son". We know that he was a very honourable man because when he discovered that Mary was pregnant and he knew that he was not the biological father, his first reaction was to spare her the shame of a public divorce. The rest we can only surmise. He was obviously a God-fearing man who wanted to do the right thing. He was prepared to accept readily the extraordinary explanation of how Mary had conceived, and he obeyed without question the instructions he received in his dream. He must have been selected quite carefully by God to be the spouse of Mary. He clearly cared for mother and child to the best of his ability; he led them to safety away from Herod's men; he raised the boy Jesus as his own son; he went searching for him when the child stayed behind teaching in the temple. I always feel that Joseph did his very best, apparently undaunted by the fact that he was required to be the stepfather of the Son of the Almighty. It would be easy to imagine how that might undermine a man's self-confidence and powers of parenting. He was quite evidently a man who had enormous trust in God.

Such devotion to God, such loving respect for his wife, such tender care for the child under his guardianship, suggests a man who would make the finest role model for all fathers.

ॐ My Lord and my God,
      may I be inspired by the loyalty, obedience
         and faithfulness of St Joseph.
      Grant that I may learn to place all my trust in you,
         understand your will for me
           and serve you with honesty and adoration.

    Lord, fill me with your grace
      so that I may be ready to receive you with joy.
        Amen.

19 December

> *"Zechariah said to the angel,*
> *'How can I be sure of this?*
> *I am an old man and my wife*
> *is getting on in years.'"*
>
> Luke 1: 18

THROUGHOUT this preparation for the birth of Christ we are being led by the Church to try and understand the importance of faith in God and His power to influence our lives, so that when He arrives we will be ready for Him. Again and again we have examples of characters in the gospels displaying their absolute faith and trust in the Lord, or indeed – as in this instance – showing doubt and misgivings. Zechariah appears to be asking for some sort of proof; he had only to wait a few months and the proof would be given to him. During the months that he lost his power of speech he had time to reflect on his error in doubting that what the Lord had said would come true. When the baby was born it was time for Zechariah to make his proclamation of faith by insisting that the boy be called 'John', as the angel had instructed, even though Zechariah's relatives were puzzled by such a name.

It is sometimes possible to fall into the trap of thinking that some trouble, hardship or illness in our lives has been inflicted on us as a punishment for something we have done which has displeased the Lord. I truly don't believe that God works like that. While He is infinitely just, He is also infinitely loving and longs to give us every chance to atone for our sins. Revenge is a very human emotion. Hardship comes our way – as it came the way of Zechariah – so that we may turn more fully towards God and observe His ability to calm our worries and ease our burdens. C.S. Lewis said, 'God whispers to us in our pleasures, speaks to us in our conscience, but shouts in our pain. It is His megaphone to rouse a deaf world.'[1]

ᘍ☛   My Lord and my God,
      grant that my faith in you may be unshakeable,
        my trust in your love for me be unmovable
         and my will to serve you be ever strong.
     Teach me to be sure always that you are with me
      in all my trials and sufferings.

    Lord, fill me with your grace
      so that I may be ready to receive you with joy.
      Amen.

---

1   *The Problem of Pain*, C.S. Lewis; Harper Collins.

20 December

'"I am the handmaid of the Lord," said Mary, "let what you have said be done to me."'

Luke 1: 38

HIS IS THE ULTIMATE in acceptance of God's will. Mary's *fiat* – 'let it be so' – is one of the most perfect prayers. She was told what would happen to her and the possibility is that she could have refused – or given in with bad grace and complaints. But God had chosen carefully; Mary had been groomed from before birth to be the perfect woman, the perfect, unstained carrier of the Son of God. She is a truly awe-inspiring role model. We have been born with the stain of original sin, and have our fallen nature with which to struggle all our lives. Nevertheless we can look at her and learn. We can see her patience and her trust. She was puzzled by what she was told – but accepted her fate and did not question Gabriel as to how she would be expected to manage, what she was supposed to say to Joseph and her friends and whether or not they would believe her. She must have known that the Son of God would have much work to do on earth – and she must have wondered how she would fit into His life and plans. But her trust in God's goodness and her certainty that He would 'sort everything out' was such that she said only 'Let what you have said be done to me.' It was the same prayer in spirit repeated by Our Lord Himself in Gethsemane: "Nevertheless, let your will be done, not mine." (Luke 22: 42)

When we pray, we often present God with lists of requests for ourselves and for those we love, we should remember Mary's and Christ's words at the end of every prayer we make.

ॐ My Lord and my God,
    I ask you to hear my prayers
        for those I care for and love,
        for those who are suffering in this world,
        and for my own intentions,
        and if it is your will please grant them.
    In all things, Almighty Father, let thy will,
        not mine, be done.

    Lord, fill me with your grace
        so that I may be ready to receive you with joy.
        Amen.

21 December

"Mary set out as quickly as she could to a town in the hill country of Judah."

Luke 1: 39

I
T'S QUITE HARD TO BELIEVE, isn't it? Such selflessness and consideration for others puts most of us to shame. Mary has just been given the momentous news that, not only is she pregnant while still a virgin, but that she is to give birth to the Son of God. This cannot have been that easy to take in and, for all her quiet acceptance of Gabriel's words and God's will, she was human and must have felt some worry. She was, after all, we assume, a young and inexperienced woman. Having been told what would happen to her, she is also told of her cousin's pregnancy – and we know that Elizabeth was 'getting on in years'. From Mary's actions, she appears not to have any thought for herself, but only for her cousin. She felt sure that Elizabeth would welcome help and company at this time, and she (in her condition) immediately crossed difficult, hilly country to go to her side to offer what support she could. Everything we know from the gospels about Mary – her kindness, compassion, consideration,

obedience, patience, acceptance of suffering and her trust in God – proves that she is worthy person for us to strive to imitate. Christ – on the cross – gave Mary to us as our mother; we should not forget to turn to her and ask for help as any child would go to his mother's side at times of pain and pleasure.

༞ Holy Mary, Queen and Mother,
            please intercede for us with Almighty God.
        Teach us humility, patience, kindness, purity,
            obedience and honesty
        and pray for us that we may accept without question
            – as you did – our Father's will for us
        and that in doing so we may reap the reward of
            meeting you one day in heaven.

    My Lord and my God, fill me with your grace
        so that I may be ready to receive you with joy.
            Amen.

22 December

"From this day forward all generations will call me blessed, for the Almighty has done great things for me."

Luke 1: 48

*O*N FIRST READING THOSE WORDS you could be forgiven for thinking that this was Our Lady being uncharacteristically boastful. 'All generations will call me blessed.' But notice that Mary immediately follows that statement by saying, "for the Almighty has done great things for me." In other words: "I shall be called 'blessed', but it has nothing to do with me – it has all to do with what God has done for me." There is a world of difference between pride and honesty. False modesty is an undesirable trait in anyone. Honesty is at the core of pure humility. We have all been given talents and gifts. To refuse to acknowledge these gifts – whether it is the ability to sing beautifully, to treat illness, to speak languages fluently, to fix cars – whatever it is – to pretend that really we are 'no good at it', or to give way to self-denigration, is an example of ingratitude to our Creator. It is He who has given us our abilities – all of them – and it is to Him that we should direct our thanks. Mary knew that she had been given a huge honour, and she knew that her name would go down in history as being the blessed Mother of God – but she also knew that it was by the grace of God that this would happen. She was merely His instrument, and her joy at being such was evident from the beautiful words of the Magnificat.

ào➡ My Lord and my God,
  I offer you my grateful thanks
    for all the many gifts you have given me.
  May I use them wisely always
    so that everything I do may be to your greater
      glory.

Lord, fill me with your grace
    so that I may be ready to receive you with joy.
      Amen.

23 December

"Stand erect, hold your heads high, because your liberation is near at hand."

Luke 21: 28

FOR FOUR WEEKS you and I have been thinking about and preparing for the arrival of this baby, the most special baby in the history of the universe. For millennia before us, mankind was waiting for this same thing. The world had descended further and further into the murkiness of sin, as man drifted further and further away from God until he was completely lost in the darkness. A star of great brightness shone in the sky 2000 years ago, to herald the brilliance of a light that was to shine on mankind for evermore. That glow which began in a stable in Bethlehem became a powerful light which swept across the world, showing man where he had gone wrong and illuminating the path he must follow back to righteousness and salvation. God, in His great love for those He had created out of love, became Man to lead us safely back to Him. Light has been shone all around us; we have been given the means by which to break free from our slavery to sin – to shake off the chains of unfaithfulness – to move freely and resolutely towards that goal for which we were created.

We have the gift of free will – only we can decide what we will do. To be enslaved to the ways of this world, or to use what we have been given to work our way towards the freedom that is God's will for us. Now is the time to hold our heads high, to be determined to change, to open our eyes to see clearly what we must do, how we can be liberated. Beware the false gaudy lights of materialism; seek only the pure light which began with the birth we celebrate tomorrow night, which continues to glow steadily throughout the pain and suffering which life can bring, and which will reach its peak of brilliance with the Resurrection into the perfect light that is the presence of God.

⁖ My Lord and my God, the time is near.
    You are now very close at hand.
    Grant that I may be ready to welcome you
        with a pure and loving heart.
    Strengthen in me the gifts
        which come from the Holy Spirit
            so that my conscience may be strong and clear,
            and my will, firm and resolute.

    Lord, fill me with your grace
        so that I may be ready to receive you with joy.
        Amen.

CHRISTMAS DAY
– A homily

I T SEEMS TO ME that every year in our secular and materialistic world the razzmatazz surrounding Christmas starts earlier and earlier. Barely have the summer sales ended when the shops begin to pack their shelves with merchandise the total value of which would solve the world's poverty problems. Town centres sparkle with tinsel and coloured lights and people rush in and out of shops like ants around an ant-hill. And this goes on for weeks: noise, selfishness and greed abound. And are people happy? Apparently, lawyers handle more divorce applications after the Christmas holiday than at any other time of the year. All the fuss and pandemonium, the revelry and over-indulgence take their toll.

And the worst of it is – most people ignore the reason why we celebrate Christmas. They've forgotten, never knew or don't care that today is the birthday of the Saviour of Mankind – their one and only hope for the sort of happiness and peace which this world and all its material goods can never offer.

You and I have been preparing for this feast for the past four weeks. But in a different way: why?

Because we have the greatest gift – that of faith. We know that we are celebrating the fact that 2000 years ago a Virgin gave birth to a wonderful child – the Son of God, the Second Person of the Blessed Trinity. It was the visible intervention of the Maker of heaven and earth. And we know that that is the only reason for all our celebrations. And yet it is largely ignored; in fact, in these days of weak, nervous and politically-correct leaders, great efforts are made to avoid making any connection between Christmas and Christian beliefs, for fear of upsetting non-believers in this, our Christian country. It's monstrous, isn't it?

But, (and it's a big 'but') we shouldn't really spend time and energy denouncing the outrageous indifference of society. Much more important to do something – however little – to compensate for such an attitude to Our Lord's arrival. It's better to light a candle than to complain of the dark.

There's a passage in the Preface for the last week of Advent expressing the hope that when Christ comes He may find us watching in prayer, our hearts filled with wonder and praise.

So as we celebrate this feast, let us give to Our Lord on His birthday, the only thing He wants from us: our hearts. Let us make a place for Him in our thinking and feeling, and give Him a much greater influence in our lives. And as you look upon the simple nativity scene depicted in the Crib, contemplate – and remind yourself that that infant is truly the great and awesome Creator of all things. That is our faith. And the response to that fact is simply to adore. Our act of faith, our acknowledgement of God's gift to us will, in a small way, make reparation for the indifference of so many.

I pray sincerely that God may bless you and all those you love – on this Christmas Day and always.

Biography

Fran was born in London. Her family lived for a few years in Southern Rhodesia (Zimbabwe), then Oxford, before settling in a village on the south coast near Bournemouth. Convent-educated Fran trained as a bi-lingual secretary, before changing tack completely and joining the local radio station in Dorset where she worked as a technical operator, commercial producer and presenter for 7 years. In 1990 Fran joined BBC Radio 2 as a newsreader/announcer – and butt of Terry Wogan's relentless teasing, for which she has been well-prepared by having two brothers and a witty punster as a father!

Profoundly grateful to her devoted mother who brought her up to be a good Catholic with firm, moral principles, Fran can nevertheless date the growth in, and transformation of, her Faith from the time she joined the parish of St James's in Spanish Place, London where she met the wise, funny, clever and deeply devout Mgr Frederick Miles, to whom she feels indebted for her spiritual awakening.

Fran lives with her laptop computer in 'a tiny flat' in central London!